DUNES REVIEW

Cover art, "Neighbors," by illustrator Trevor Grabill.

DUNES REVIEW (ISSN: 1545-3111) is published biannually by
Michigan Writers, Inc., and with the generous contributions of our Patrons.

It costs about $40 to produce one page of Dunes Review.

We welcome Patrons. Send your check payable to Michigan Writers to:
Michigan Writers, P.O. Box 2355, Traverse City, MI 49685

Your support is greatly appreciated.

DUNES REVIEW

VOLUME 18, ISSUE II

CONTENTS

Editor's Note

Sometimes we hope things will happen even though we're fairly sure they never will. It's not that some events are impossible; there is always a chance of windfall, lottery, a serendipitous something or other. Likelihood is set aside for the simple pleasure of hoping. At times our hope is so deeply planted, so much a part of our very being that we can't escape it. Yet fruition is beside the point. The idea is to continue looking up.

But hope doesn't always feel good. The weight of opposite possibility bears down, reality's gravity rooting us firmly to the ground. Still, our eyes gaze heavenward, open to receive, expectant.

The pieces in this issue pull me in both directions: the anticipation of a young boy's elk hunt in an essay on wilderness alongside empty chairs strewn about in the kitchen, foreshadowing certain loss. Tender moments beneath a serenade of meteors are balanced by the weight of a fading grandmother. We exist always in the space between hope and anti-hope, each extreme a source of mystery. It is a challenge to embrace the uncertainty, to appreciate the magic of everything beyond our reach and lines of sight, but often that uncertainty is all we have.

Stretch up, sink down. Then stand in the balance.

—Jennifer Yeatts

Amy Schmidt
TO THE POT OF DEAD FLOWERS AFTER WINTER HAS RECEDED

All through this season I thought maybe I would be the one to die.

It's a relief, then, to see you.

By your body, brittle needs no definition; your cracked
soil is a sigh. The surroundings swallow
you, vanishing your parts into tufts of grass
that have not found their color yet. You are ugly
and because of this, many people have walked
right past, seeing only the shapes between
your withered stems. They will go on un-seeing, passing
into the spaces between molecules of air in search
of spring.

But I've considered your situation: the roots are buried
but still breathing; the husk of winter has no choice
in its receding.

By your body, mine feels strangely more alive.

KAREN ANDERSON
BELIEVING

Twist of snow off garage
roof. Kitchen shears
    snap crush
cutting stems of mums
fibrous stalk swollen end
    believing
this will extend their life.

Pale yellow blossoms deep
purple fringed eyes shining
    not for me.

Cold white against
my window. Paring knife
    peels releases
chopping garlic cloves
into lentil soup buds of fire
    believing
this will heal everything.

Once I apologized for garlic
on my fingers. You put them
    in your mouth.

Between two hungry
seasons waiting
    for the light
    to change
you to smear garlic
    stir me
        cut my stems.

Kevin Oberlin
MEMORY OF SAGINAW, NO RETURN ADDRESS

If I was the slight teenage boy who stood
on the corner outside your house and skipped rocks
across the street and into your hedge, I would
like to apologize for that. I've taken stock
of the women I've failed to love, and you were the worst:
the notes slipped into your folder (which you returned),
stolen socks, the amorous looks rehearsed
to raise your boyfriend's ire once I'd learned
he was prone to violent self-abuse, and the milk
I left in your locker over the long weekend.
I embarrassed you out of love, though now I think
the stink proves there was little there to commend.
Even if you had called, I couldn't explain
the clenched heart's patience, its skew and strain.

Rebecca Pelky
RESERVATION LOVE STORY

Ours was a Boonesfarm kind of love,
a brown bag and corner store sort;

a speck of dust turned significant
when it made us sneeze.

It was a late winter thing, the cold
keeping up, close; tulips, too distracting.

Fingers digging under old denim
behind the smokehouse, in the warm

flumes of salmon or rabbit,
where mosquitos let us alone, for a while.

That was the spring I was snow-blind,
and no goldenseal poultice could cure me.

I'd found your good red road,
your shielding aspen, slipped and faded

like northern lights across April. You pulled
22 ticks from my pale places, the soft spots

behind my knees, the small of my back,
that night we waded the cedar swamp

to see meteors in perfect dark, begged
on each one, as if it would keep us.

Amy Schmidt
ORACLE OF ARACHNID

> "...the spider may indicate that the dreamer is being
> manipulated..."   —Cynthia Richmond, *Dream Power*

In Spain, she recklessly fell in love with a boy
whose name translated to Little Fat Easter Ham.
In the kitchen of azure tiles, he fed her
negra arroz, the splendid ink of the cuttlefish staining
each grain of rice dark as the ocean's bottom. Sizzling
and spattering in hot oil, each tentacle succumbed
to garlic and paprika, the sweet sting of the Cubanelle
pepper and slowly, she did the same, soaking up
the smooth simmer of his laugh, the sound of her
name, Julia, filling the air with such lightness
she began to think him splendid enough to change
the properties of oxygen.

Together they hiked to a gazebo made of glass.
Below them, Granada spilled across the foothills
of the Alpujarra like a handful of washed stones.
Toasting thin stemmed glasses of wine, cheap
but from Riojas, they watched night wash over
the roofs and monastery spires like foamy waves.
They fell asleep on the slat board floor. Tangled
in his arms, she dreamt about spiders, hoards
of them crowding the walls and ceiling of the room.
They spoke their strange language urgently, their
impossibly small mandibles smacking against
a great stillness. The moon pilfered
what bits of space it could find between
the legs, abdomens and palps, its rays
like pinpoint stars in a sky of trembling black.

When she woke she could think of nothing
but the words she could not understand.
Had she a translation, a familiar tense, even a hint
of context to follow. Air, they'd said, is air. Alter that
and all will fail.

Joey Kingsley
DOVETAIL

O such woe: I broke my last Marlboro, me being one of two
in a pact to surrender the stupid things. Between the ends,
crinkled tobacco falls. Last week, I remembered
the chandelier that crashed in a crescendo, the phantom
disappearing backstage, unmasked. The Station burned
that night. Across town, the band's pyrotechnics
ignited exposed sound insulation in the ceiling. It'd be a lie
to say I felt guiltless in black, matching time to place.

At the point of no return, I recall my great-grandfather's
ashtray, raised skeleton head a reminder that even
the neighbor's weed whacker in its whirring whine
of blades is beheading the very life that gives life.
Outside, I plant a double row of mammoth sunflowers,
scoop pockets of soil out with a spoon & into the dark
drop the seeds. Across the street, a woman prunes a tree & fills
three buckets with peach blossoms. A couple in the park
begins to disappear as shadows drift over them.
The flowers, helpless to hang on, let go their petals.

The truth: giving up what kills me kills me.
Passing a house with a birdcage hanging from the porch,
a hot-pink plastic bird wobbles a branch
beyond the rusty door. I'd set it free, but I gave up
impulsivity for Lent. And on the back of an Alzheimer's
seminar evaluation, my aunt's letter arrives from Long Island.
How well did the presenter identify the learning objectives?
Too boring. She says my cousin is living at home again,
seeing a new girl. Last Saturday, the cab driver told me
a woman went to get cash at an ATM & skipped out on her fare,
leaving her purse in the backseat. She never returned.

Inside: a wad of napkins, two liters of Coke.
Last week, I fell asleep to a film about a dream within
a dream. The actors wander the streets of each other's minds.
Right here, I tell the cabbie. When I lived in another city,
a tall man used to press his mouth to the veins inside my wrist.
He smoked down to the filter. At the airport, he lifted

his bags, thin as a string bean. The idea is to leave & come back.
The cabbie said, pay the meter, or you'll break my heart.

David Hardin
BLANK

Father was a quarryman, hands at home
On a welded wheel, fingers stiff, waiting for sun
To clear the lip of the pit, an artist is his own way

Content to read the grain through an emery palm
Leaving the rest to rain and wind. Mother on the other
Hand was a chiseler with a syncopated mallet

No stranger to the fluter and veiner, fine dust felting
Her coffee, laboring late, ankle deep in drifting flake
Humming as she whittled to the quick.

This morning, seeing my chance, right hand freed
In the wee, wee hours, I hacked out feet and a face
Only a mother could love, raking footprints clean as I left.

LISA WAMSLEY
INDIAN SUMMER

You don't know Indian Summer when you're six
    how the dazzling sky and white clouds
        are any different, or more precious, than June's

And you don't know how an ordinary day
    can amend the promise of consistency
        until it does

One moment, your neighbor is your neighbor
    then he's standing at the bottom of your driveway
        telling you you can't go into your own house

You eat cookies on his davenport
    wondering about the ambulance
        wailing through the neighborhood earlier that afternoon

When they open the front door
    you fly like a bird from a stovepipe
        straight to your own kitchen

Empty chairs in random places
    the living room a space of
        shag orange stillness

Sobs leak from behind the bedroom door
    knock knock. turn the handle. locked. knock.
        door opens just enough

Dim and dark and humid
    some sister's face between door and jamb
        "Dad's dead. He died. Go sit in the living room."

You sit and wait
    bees bounce against screens
        you want a bologna sandwich

You sit and watch
    people come and go
        the funeral takes place without you.

You sit
    in the cursory warmth
        with paltry clouds

No one comes
    Indian summer
        in a single October afternoon.

Elizabeth Arnold
SHOT IN THE DARK
Lower Camp—Bridger-Teton Wilderness—October 2010

Five a.m. still dark in the thickness of timber. I am alone on this side of the mountain except for the horse under me, and the four I'm ponying back to camp. Below us I know streams of light begin to fill the valley where we are camped, cutting through haze and mist and landing in flashes across the water. I'm trying not to think about the light breaking below us. I'm trying to think about anything but this shifting darkness and the fact that, at this moment, I have no idea where I am.

Last night C.J. and Karl decided that in the morning they would ride with the hunters a few miles into the mountains and hunt back toward camp on foot. Which means my job as camp wrangler is to ride along and bring the horses back.

When C.J. and Karl decided to hunt on foot, the hunters, a father and son from Louisiana, seemed leery of trekking so far at this altitude. Though barely fifty and seemingly fit, the Father often takes breaks walking between the tents in camp—a relatively small spread fourteen miles into the backcountry of the Bridger-Teton wilderness. Camp's not two hundred yards from one end to the other, with only a few tents—the cook tent, two hunter tents and the guide tent where the guys and I sleep. We're situated along a riverbank, surrounded on all sides by sharp ridges and shadowy tree lines. A small fire circle sits on the north edge, the corrals just beyond it. He always stops with his palm planted on his back, his head tilted toward the sky as if wanting, all of a sudden, to study the clouds. His boy, blue-eyed with brown hair trimmed short, seems small for his age at thirteen and doesn't say much; he keeps his eyes down in what seems to be nervousness, content to let his Father do the talking. Back at the trailhead, when I'd introduced him to his horse, Big Ben, he listened carefully to my instructions and did everything exactly as I said. He responds to the three of us with yes ma'am and no sir. Normally that would impress me; instead I sense a sadness behind his polite replies. I wonder if his life consists of a litany of strangers like me giving instructions. This morning he will be the one to make the first shot should they see an elk, or so his Father told us all proudly at breakfast. As we saddled together in the dark, our headlights bouncing from the horses' backs to one another's faces, Karl said that the day before was the first he'd shot the Blaser R93 Bolt-Action Rifle his Father bought for their trip together. Karl said he'd held the gun stiffly, unsure of how to press the safety, or of how much pressure it would take to pull the trigger.

As he talked, I envisioned the gun's polished barrel glimmering in the morning sun as the boy aimed uneasily at a painted hay-bale. I could imagine his body shaking as the butt of the gun connected with his shoulder, his ears pounding with the power of the shot. I'm sure that to them this seems like the greatest of possible adventures—a week in the mountains, a real wilderness excursion, and a chance for this slight, quiet boy to prove himself a man.

I think the guys knew I was afraid the moment they dismounted and pulled their guns free. Their voices came in whispers as they tied the horses nose to tail, hard and fast to the saddle horn ahead so that the four horses were tied in a line, connected to one another. They gave me instructions as they worked: watch that they don't take the wrong way around trees and hook the scabbards, go slow, try to make them wait for each other to get over the deadfall. I'd like to think they spoke so softly because they were worried about me, but probably they didn't want to scare off the elk. The three of us have worked together nearly every day for the past five months. C.J. and Karl are in their early twenties, a few years younger than me, but they've both grown up in the mountains and know this landscape better than anyone. Karl's almost six feet tall, trim and dark-complected with brown hair and eyes. C.J. stands well over six feet, his childlike face and bright green eyes might make you question his experience, but he's more capable than many men twice his age. Karl stood with the hunters, pointing toward the next ridge as C.J. handed me the lead to his big, half-draft gelding, Peter. He placed a gloved fist on my knee, "We'll see you back at camp."

I nodded.

He told me to follow the mountain down until I hit the trail, light would come soon. He looked up at me. "Do you know where you are?"

I bit my lip, adjusting the cuffs of my coat over my gloves as I shook my head, no.

"The horses do, you'll be fine."

I heeled my horse Cash, ready to go, when C.J. turned back, pressed my knee again, and said, "Try not to make too much noise." He grinned and turned in the direction Karl had taken the hunters.

So here we are the horses and me, beginning to make our way back, only yards from where C.J. left us and already he's gone and we are alone in the cold dark trying to pick our way between the tight spaces of trees and over a maze of lumbering deadfall down this trail-less mountainside. I hold Cash's reins in my left hand and Peter's lead in my right. I just have to hope that the leads connecting the three horses behind Peter don't give and leave me with a mess scattered across the mountainside.

The frozen air closes in around us. I lean back in the saddle and tighten my grip on Peter's lead. If I drop it I will have to stop, step to the ground and pick it up, which, at this moment is my greatest fear. I feel safe above the ground, safe so long as Cash's ears point forward in the confidence that at least he knows where we're going. I lean forward to duck under branches, my face against his neck, and inhale the warm strength of him.

The leather on the empty saddles moans against the cold, creaking like the branches breaking under the horses' feet. I can barely see beyond the fuzzy tips of Cash's ears and the small clouds of his breath. It's so much harder than I imagined, taking them slow and keeping watch for the clearest path ahead while shifting every few strides to make sure they follow close. I pull on the reins and ask Cash to take smaller strides so as to give the horses behind time to pick their way. They're anxious; I feel it in the roundness of their eyes, the quickness of their breath as the leads connecting them tighten and give while hips and shoulders rock in their awkward downhill gait.

I want to pull my hat farther down on my ears, but don't. The smallest movement seems dangerous as if it might bring attention to us, and I feel so large and so small at the same time, wholly alone in the world and wholly exposed to the danger of the horses spooking and throwing me, leaving me alone and on foot in a timber so thick I wouldn't see a bear until it was on top of me. So I sit still as I can and focus on the horses and the trees beside and below us, the only things separating us from the trail I'm praying we'll find. I try not to question why I am here, but I can't help it. I don't know one other woman in my family who would do this. My boyfriend safe in his life back East, doesn't say much about it, but tells me he could never do it. I know, even though he's never said it, that he's afraid for me.

When people ask me why I want to ride fifteen miles into the back country and wrangle in camp—a job almost always taken by men—I'm not sure what to tell them, except that I struggle with this desire to experience the wild, and to not be afraid of all it holds secret. It was easy, back at the ranch, to laugh at the guys when they told me girls don't belong in camp and tell them I would show them, I would not screw up.

Maybe what I fear most is looking back at my life ten years from now, from the safety of a nice house, a nice husband, and a few nice kids—a place where I've forgotten what it means to look into the darkness behind a tree-line and shudder—to feel panic rise smooth and round as a stone from belly to throat—reminding me of the life I must protect— and then saying, I wish I would have been brave enough to take a shot at the backcountry.

Talking to the horses in my head helps me stay calm so I fall into a rhythm, saying over and over again, good job boys, we're almost there boys, watch your step boys. Their strides feel careful, purposeful, as if they know I need them to do this right as much as they need me to lead them home.

Fog rises like ghosts through the trees, in apparitions of my fear —a wolf standing gray against the dark space ahead, his cool, steely eyes boring into our horseflesh caravan. Sound moves through darkness like the fog and I think I hear something huffing. I'm sure it's a grizzly snout pointed skyward, breathing us in.

The timber grows more dense and I'm afraid I've taken a wrong path, but there's no way to turn around without getting stuck. We weave under and between branches. Everything happens too slow or too fast; either we're creeping down this hillside so slowly I think we will never get back, or one of the horses gets himself hung up on a sapling, or refuses to step over a log and sits back against the pull of the line, flailing furiously for what feels like minutes in which I'm reduced to whispered prayers of—come on come on come on—feeling completely helpless and aware of every sound we make.

My inner voice begins to whisper that we're going the wrong way. This stand of trees does not look like one we passed before. Surely we're not headed downhill, but across in the wrong direction. I inhale and the air is a blade in my throat. Already I wish I'd paid more attention as we rode up this side of the mountain. Just go down C.J. said, but the hill slopes more than it falls, and down seems like a relative term. Somewhere in the distance an elk bugles, his song high and haunted. Though I'm not sure if it's real, or Karl's call. My body braces in the saddle, my grip on Peter's lead tight, waiting for a shot, ready for the horses to spook. All summer I begged our boss Jesse to let me wrangle in camp. Now I'm wondering why, knowing I could be managing the rides from the lodge, giving orders to a crew of cowboys, sleeping safe and comfortable at night. No one would have thought less of me for not coming to hunting camp or backing out and riding home—in fact they might think me more sane. This morning feels like madness, as if it's not me in this saddle but some other girl trying to prove she belongs in these woods.

When the shot rings out it's me that spooks, not the horses. My breath catches and for a moment my fingers stop quivering. Somewhere on the other side of this mountain an elk has most likely been hit. Ahead I can see the ground leveling out, maybe a hint of the trail. If I squint I can almost make out places of light to the east. The number of logs across our trail has dwindled making it easier for us. Cash's step quickens, his ears prick. I know the trail must be close, but Peter's lead pulls and I slow him, wondering about the boy, wondering if he's doing this only to please his father. Did he really want to pull the trigger when he placed the animal in his sights? How could he know what it would mean to see the elk catch and jerk, careen down through the timber, slender legs buckling, eyes wide, its wild heart splitting in two?

***

Lynnae, the camp cook, finds me reading in my tent at noon. "Lunch?" She asks. On our walk to the cook tent we see figures in the distance, four of them. I'd been right, it was the boy who made the shot, a bull elk they'd seen not thirty minutes after leaving me. The Father grasped the boy's shoulder as he told us, waving the end of his gun with his free hand as he pointed to the spot, behind us, where they'd first seen him. The elk had been hit, that much they knew. The blood trail was solid and easy to follow at first, but then thinned, tapered off and disappeared with no sign of the elk, meaning probably that the shot was bad and the elk was only wounded. This is the outcome guides and hunters hate. An animal shot clean and correct means a quick death and a filled tag. A botched shot leaves an animal hurt and dying slowly, sometimes impossible to find. The look on the boy's face as he listens to Karl describing the blood trail and their search tells me he understands all of this.

We eat lunch in silence for the most part. Across from me, at the long slab of table in the cook tent, the Father's face shines flushed and sweating as he tells us about the parties he throws for the other partners in the firm, and the number of maids he employs. The boy does little more than push the potatoes back and forth through his stew. Karl decides that he's going to go back out with his dog after lunch and hope he might help pick up the lost trail.

***

It's close to dark with everyone sitting on logs and stumps around the fire when Karl finally walks back into camp, the dog trails him, tongue lolling. It surprises all of us when the boy speaks up first. "Did you find him?"

When Karl shakes his head, the boy's Father pats his back once. "Don't worry, we'll find you another one."

The boy leans toward the light of the fire, claps his knees and the dog ambles over, happy to be rubbed and scratched on the neck. "Do you think he smelled anything?" he asks Karl.

"Oh, he smells everything; but he didn't pick up any trails."

Lynnae tells Karl she saved him supper and as they walk toward the cook tent I move over toward the boy and sit down next to him, still rubbing the dog's thick neck. Part of me wishes Karl would sense what I do in the boy and make something up, some hint that the elk is okay, or will be found. Earlier today Lynnae placed the fixings for a campfire treat behind our log seats and I reach for the box of graham crackers, a bag of marshmallows, and a few Hershey bars which have melted and re-formed. C.J. sees me and gets up. I know he's going to cut willow branches along the river.

Our marshmallows glow against the dark, everyone sitting around the fire again and Karl scraping stew from a tin plate propped on his knee, giving the dog every third or fourth bite. The camp has grown quiet except for the pops of the fire and the dog's slurping. I think no one wants to talk about the day or plan for the next when Karl starts, his slow Montana accent—not quite a drawl and not quite Canadian—rolling into one of his stories, so famous around the ranch's campfires. He says, "My grandfather knew this outfitter north of Helena, did elk hunts like ours. Well, he got these two guys in for an early season elk hunt—bow hunt. They were a father and son. Now, the son had been bow hunting for a long time, was a great shot. He'd won long-range archery contests, the whole deal. His dad on the other hand had never shot a bow in his life, maybe once, I don't know, but he wasn't the shot his son was. Anyhow they both had tags and they were both going to try to take a bull with a bow. So these guys go out the first morning in camp—on foot, no guide. They're from Bozeman and they know the mountains. They've been walking close to an hour, and it's probably not quite light yet when they come on what looks like an old wolf-kill. They're creeping around it, trying to get out of there when out of nowhere this Grizz charges, and he doesn't stop. He takes out the son, knocks him down and sends him flying almost a hundred yards down this hill they just climbed, and the Grizz is right after him. The son tries to get up and he knocks him down again and just starts gnawin' on him. So the dad's still up at the top of the hill, watchin' this bear tear his son apart. You know what he does?"

Karl waits as if we'll answer, but no one does. We're all riveted, even C.J., even the dog. "He pulls off his bow, puts an arrow on, sights up, draws, and lets it go." Karl pauses, tilts his plate, scrapes it up and down, fills his fork. "That arrow flies straight down the hill and clean through that old bear's heart. Kills him in an instant."

"Did the guy live?" C.J. asks.

"Oh yeah," Karl says, chewing. "He was tore up pretty bad, but he made it."

I hand the boy a graham cracker, then a piece of chocolate. He presses them onto a waiting marshmallow. Together we listen as Karl, C.J., and the boy's father go on about Karl's story, about what a man that Montana father was. The boy and I sit that way for a while, chewing and toeing our crumbs toward the fire. He leans over toward me, asks, just loud enough for me to hear, "Do you think the elk is suffering?"

I exhale, and purse my lips, knowing that he's probably been fixating on this question since it happened. I lean over and throw my last bite into the fire. I can tell he wants an honest answer. "Well, I don't know. There's probably a good chance he's already dead. He might have lost a lot of blood." I pause, look over at him and his eyes meet mine for the first time. "I'm guessing the wolves have gotten him. Nature has a way of working these things out."

Later, as we're leaving the fire, the Father takes C.J.'s arm and whispers something. C.J. nods a few times and says, "Yep, yep, okay." The guys wait outside our tent while I change into fresh long underwear and slip between the still-cold flannel of my sleeping bag. Once I yell out that it's safe for them to come in Karl adds a few pieces of wood to the tent stove and C.J. laces the flaps closed. Dakota turns around and around scratching at the bottom of Karl's bag. I'm reading by the light of my headlamp while they undress down to their union suits and crawl into the bags on either side of me. Everything is still, quiet and almost dark, save the stove's licks of fire, when I ask C.J. what the father wanted. He sighs and says they want to ride out tomorrow and hunt from the lodge. Karl grunts. I ask him if he's surprised and he says no, that he thinks it's the Dad's idea more than the kids, that he just wants his boy to shoot an elk. C.J. says that the boy doesn't seem to care one bit. He adds, "His poor arm was shaking like a leaf when he took that shot."

***

Almost one in the afternoon the next day, the warmest in camp so far, with the sun high over the valley's east ridge and a powder blue sky. That morning I'd turned the horses loose to roam the meadows around camp, leaving Cash tied near my tent to retrieve them later.

Finally, I'm beginning to feel at ease here, at least in the daylight. My heart has adjusted to the rhythm of this place, to the slowness of the days and the even slower nights. Life in the wilderness moves at an animal pace, days dictated by the needs of the horses, the mules and the animals we hunt. My body has taken on a tension, a strength I feel in the coil of each muscle, the quick lighting of my eyes over this landscape. Night falls and the cries of cougars and wolves remind us of where we sit in the hierarchy of the wild, the relativity of the word hunt.

I find the horses two clearings east of camp, a few mules drinking from the river, the white Percheron pack mare, Bell, lying up on her sternum in meadow grass, either too lazy or too content to stand and eat. The herd for the most part ignores me. A few ears prick and flicker in my direction, but I can tell they're hoping I'll leave them alone. My calls of, "hey boys, let's go home boys," and one crack of the whip wake the sleeping and send the mules splashing onto the riverbank. Bell heaves her great body from the ground, shakes like a dog and breaks into a trot. They fall into line and I follow, thinking about the hunters' long ride out this afternoon, and about the boy— whom I think wishes to be brave in the same ways I do—about all the reasons his Father brought him here, and all the reasons they are going home.

I follow the horses, considering my days in camp, the fact that they are numbered. I leave in five days, and in my heart I know I'm living my last days, ever, in this kind of wilderness. In a few months I'll return to my life back east. None of this will matter then—not my ability to help the guys fall a tree with a cross-cut saw, or dally it against the horn of my saddle as Cash and I drag it into camp, not my willingness to wake in the dark with only the light of my headlamp and sort horses from mules in a make-shift corral, not even the way I crack the bull-whip calling every four-limbed thing within earshot to attention. I post to the rhythm of Cash's quick strides, knowing what the measure of my life might soon be. It's my choice, I know, to leave this job and go back to my life with my boyfriend. I imagine our lives will move in the steady, quiet rhythm of a garden in summer, warm eggs gathered in wicker baskets, and winter's slow-burning fires. But at this point in my life—after college and a graduate degree—as I'm about to leave the calculated pause of this job, I know that returning to that other life means entering the world of women which carries ancient questions. Will she get married? Will she have a baby? Will she use her body for what it's intended, designed?

Cash skitters on the trail, a leaf blows past us but I keep my seat. Why must we measure the worth of our lives this way? Why can't the measure of my life be this—that yesterday I felt as alone and afraid as I ever had, but I managed to lead four horses off a mountain in the dark and find my way home.

***

I scattered grain and hay pellets through the corral earlier so the horses trot straight in. Karl and C.J. work at filling their saddlebags, slipping

their rifles into the scabbards on their saddles when they ask me to find
the boy. They're just about ready to leave and Lynnae's gone to wake
the Father who's been asleep in the tent since lunch. When I don't
find him at the fire ring or the cook tent, my breath catches and pace
quickens. A million scenarios run through my mind. When is the last
time anyone saw him? I'm thinking about the bear Lynnae saw days
ago, before we arrived, not two hundred yards from here, and the
cougar's den we know is close because we've heard their screams. Has
he wandered too far past camp and gotten himself turned around, lost?
I pull back the flap to our guide tent, then Lynnae's, then the cook tent.
Nothing. My steps quicken and my leather-soled boots slip along the
river's edge as I call his name. Only a raven responds. A surge of fear
rises until I hear a sound in the distance.

I find him along the river, a few hundred yards down, throwing
stones. He's hopping from rock to rock on the bank and stops to fling a
stone level from the wrist. It skips once, then drops. The next he hauls
overhand and it lands with a loud plunk and splash near the river's
deep center. I stop for a moment and watch, arms folded across my
chest. I need to tell him it's time to leave but I want to say so much
more. If I could I'd place my arm around his narrow shoulders and
tell him not to worry too much about what happened on the side of
the mountain, not about the elk, or the miss, or the suffering. I want
to tell him to remember his horse and the feel of his sure, even strides
as they leave this place, to remember the s'mores and the campfire and
his first night sleeping on the ground. I want to tell him to remember
this day and these rocks, the quick plop and splash as they entered the
river and the water that rushed to cover them. I want to remind him,
more than anything of his bravery, of the bravery of the elk that is now
somewhere dying, hopefully already dead.

***

Two days from now father and son will be eating warm, comfortable
meals from the lodge and riding over the crest of two small hills to sit and
wait for a bull the lodge guides have scouted. C.J. and Karl will be back in
camp with new hunters. These men will be experienced, so I shouldn't be
surprised when they want to hunt until dark their first night in camp.

I'll go along to bring the horses back. When we reach the top of a boggy
clearing and cross into the timber single file Karl, in the lead, will yell,

"Hey. Whoa. Hey, bear. Get out of here, bear!" The horses will start to dance underneath us and my heart will stop for what feels like thirty-full seconds until Karl looks back and says, "He's gone." My leg will begin to shake in sewing machine fashion against Cash's side as his legs cross and uncross, sinking into the soft earth. I'll lean down and tell him it's okay, wishing he could say it back. Instead his head will bob and his lips will flutter to the rhythm of his feet, horse-spit flying. Soothing him won't work to shift my thoughts from the bear. In my mind it's a huge boar, cinnamon and strong with eyes black as onyx, wanting to charge. My visions make it hard to refrain from looking over my shoulder every few seconds, then scanning the ground below us, waiting for the beast to circle back around.

Turns out we've interrupted the bear in the process of eating a bull elk carcass he'd buried under branches, pine needles and loamy forest ground. When Karl and C.J. step off their horses they'll hand me their reins, leaving the hunters—guns drawn—and me, still watching for the bear to come back. I'll press Cash as close to the trees' edge as he'll go, not so I can see what the guys see, but so I will be close to them. In the almost dark, hunched over the bear's meat mound, they'll talk in low whispers while pushing branches away and pulling the rotting carcass from the ground. I'll manage to hear, "Looks like the kid's," and "would be about the right place."

They'll cover it quickly and walk backward to where I hold the horses, somehow managing to keep my horse, in his fear, from tangling in their rigs. Riding away, when Cash's neck has finally lowered, relaxed and I, again, feel safe, I'll ask C.J. if he thinks the elk is the one the boy wounded.

"Probably," he'll say. "Rack is the right size. Karl and me will come back in the morning if the bear's gone and get the antlers, give 'em to the kid. He'll probably want to have 'em."

"Yes," I'll say. "He probably will."

PATRICK KINDIG
STILL LIFE IN THE SPACE BETWEEN TWO DEATHS

There's a mound of ladybug shells on the windowsill and
I've hung popcorn around my throat like a necklace.
The day's bowl of wind rises outside and I try to sketch

a portrait of habit: first a pebble in the heel of a shoe, then
a horse, then the white thread at the heart of a handmade
bracelet. None of these seems correct so I count

marigold seeds with my fingers and drink a sixth cup
of coffee. My nails split the skin of an orange
and the world spills out, stretching like molten glass

past all mathematical limits. The sky becomes a tepid
reflecting pool. I hold my breath and slip my toe
through its meniscus. No, that can't be right—I throw

my whole body through like an anchor made of rice paper.

MERCEDES LAWRY
THE LITTLE SOFT FEET OF THE NIGHT

Creep, creep, the effortless and the damned.
Wind drags the paper bag across the walk
and over and back, trailing a scuttle of leaves.
No one hears the hiss.
Crows scissor the sky as the light goes,
sift and blink. Quiet and hush.
The harmed are locked clean away
with no evidence. Out of the picture,
thieves and beggars, babies and gods.
What comes to bear goes missing
with the fugitive moon. Lack and bemoan.

BRANDYN JOHNSON
HONEYSUCKLES

Deep in their roots, all flowers keep the light. —Theodore Roethke

We snuck through woods we weren't supposed to pass
until we found a honeysuckle wall: pearl & maize & emerald & cotton.

Each one plucked was a tiny fire dissolving into our tongues.
Discarded petals gathered in piles at our feet like counted stars.

Still the wall lost no shine. Bells hollered over the treetops,
calling us back. We ignored. We became hummingbirds.

We became yellowjackets. Our tongues, fingers sticky.
Sunlight ticked across the sky. All the while we knew

we were in trouble. We simulated something we didn't know
we knew how to do. That first taste frisson I keep in my roots,

a dream that is still plowing its way through the clouds.

Dixon Hearne
PETTY WISE

"Tell that boy to get down off that crate, Miss Sally—unless you want to pay for it. I done told him once. Them crates are easy broke." Mr. Crouch ain't happy with us. Mama give me a hard look, and I do what he say. He tell Mama that Miss Petty say I got sticky fingers—said I stole a candy bar one time. Miss Petty, she work the store most of the time, but she ain't no more friendly than him. Mr. Crouch, he own the store and get all the business from colored quarters and don't never give nothin' away. Old man Boudreaux over in Tallulah, he give me a piece of gum or hard candy sometime when I go to his store with Granny. But not Mr. Crouch or Miss Petty.

Mama say I'm too young to know, but I see plain as day that man's tryin' to cheat us out the price it say in the window. He tell mama she can't read and that's a lie. I know some words, too, and it say right there: "Chicken Necks .29/lb." I been totin' stuff home from this store for two years. I know the price on lots of things, and I know them chicken necks is .29 a pound. And I ain't goin' let it go till he sell it for that. We come all this way on bare feet and hot Mississippi dirt and got to walk back now—we ain't leavin' without what we come for. Sunday's dumplin' day and we got to have them necks for it, even if they skinny and small.

Mama sets some of her things on the counter and we go lookin' for what's left on her list: cocoa, sugar, corn meal—things we don't grow. Mr. Crouch, he keep his eye popped wide on us—'specially me. I ain't never stole nothin' from his store, and it make me mad inside that Miss Petty say I did. Make me mad too that the man ain't said nothin' to them other two mamas and they children shoppin' in the store with us. We know them from the quarter, and they say hi to us. One boy, Martel, him and me play marbles in the yard, but he bad to cheat. He don't talk to me, and I don't care. Some bananas in a basket got my eye right now and make me think about Mama's nana puddin'.

By the time we ready to pay for the groceries and bag them up, Mama done lost patience with Martel's Mama. She just shove our groceries way off to the side and start piling her rice sack and salt and Luzianne tea ahead of us on the counter—and she ain't even through with her shoppin'.

26

"Y'all ready, Miss Sally?" old man Crouch ask. "Ain't no specials in your groceries today."

I tell him again 'bout the chicken necks, and he say they ain't had time to change the sign. I don't believe him. First he say Mama can't read, and now he tell us this. I think he means them necks is .29/lb. for everybody 'cept folks in the quarter. That's what I think. But before I can say so, Mama give me another cold look and my mouth stays shut.

"Three dollars and ninety-four cents," Mr. Crouch say, not smilin' or friendly at all. "Ya'll got to learn to come early in the morning. You come in here sweating and smelling up my whole store."

The other Mamas hear what the man say and look straight at us. They sweaty, too, and got sweaty children with them. But it ain't no way folks can get away from they mornin' field work to buy groceries, 'cept on Sunday—and he ain't open then. We all stare at the man, but he don't even look up from countin' his money and smokin' his Lucky Strike. Mama quick bag up everything in the pillow case she brung from home, and we hurry out the door, wishin' we could leave all the hate behind us. But them other mamas, they got to be told the same mean thing when they check out.

*

Mama and me take turns totin' the heavy load on the hot walk home. Everybody settin' and fannin' on they front porch when we straggle in. But it won't last long—back to the fields after they rest. And Lord it's hot when we get back and start unloadin' the groceries. Flies is followed us every step of the way and right on in the house. Ain't got enough swatters to kill them all.

"Get my boiler out there, Jackson," Mama tell me, "the big one with the broke handle." She got to get supper goin' 'fore she leave for the fields again. All I gots to do is keep an eye on it like she tell me and turn the fire out at 5:00 by the little clock on the counter. I help Mama cook every day at the same time—mostly peas or beans with fatback or hocks. But Sunday is always dumplin' day and Daddy nearly eat the whole pot.

Come 4:30 by the clock, I hear a loud rap on the door. It ain't usually shut in the summertime, but somebody in the quarter is burnin' trash and the smoke keep comin' through the screen. I open the door and find Sheriff Baxter and Mr. Crouch standin' there on the porch. Mr. Crouch, he still puffin' on a Lucky Strike and coughin'.

"Jackson, is your Mama in there?" Sheriff Baxter ask me. "I need to talk to her."

"Naw sir," I say back to him. "She out in the fields."

"Which fields is she workin' today, boy?" Mr. Crouch ask me, real mean-like.

"Pickin' peas I 'spect," I say. "Why come you need to talk to her?"

"We'll tell that to your Mama," the Sheriff say back to me. "We'll be back soon."

The two of them tear off down the dirt road toward the fields and I'm gettin' worried now. Mama ain't done nothin' wrong. And Daddy, he workin' some fields way over in Delhi.

I go cross the road to Miss Ebbie's house and tell her 'bout it, and she take me back home and stay with me till Sheriff Baxter and Mr. Crouch finally come ridin' back up and drag Mama out the back seat. By now, all the old men and women that can't work the fields no more are starin' and pointin' from they porches.

"We got some talking to do, Jackson," Sheriff Baxter say to me. "Mr. Crouch here says you stole a candy bar from his store today. A PayDay. Did you eat it already?"

Mama wiggle loose and come to my side. She say, "Jackson ain't stole nothin' from your store, Mr. Crouch. Not today or never." She hug me close to her. "You watched us the whole time we was shoppin'. Did you see him take that candy bar, Mr. Crouch?"

"Boy's sneaky," the man say. "Selma Petty says she has to watch that boy close every time you send him to the store." He push his hat back on his head and stare me in the eye. "Jackson, that candy bar only cost a nickel. But it's stealing whether it's a nickel or a hundred dollars."

"Give the boy a chance to answer, Warren," the Sheriff says to the man. "You don't know why he took it." Sheriff looks right at me and says: "Why'd you take that candy bar, Jackson? You hungry? Don't your mama here feed you right?"

"I ain't stole nothin', I say back to him. "Maybe he done ate it. Maybe Miss Selma, she done ate it." I feel a madness growin' in my head and my heart beatin' loud. "Could of been Martel took it. He was right there too."

"I'm afraid we got to take your mama down to the courthouse, son," Sheriff Baxter say. He turn to Miss Ebbie and say, "You keep an eye on this boy till his daddy gets home." He put handcuffs on Mama then say to Miss Ebbie, "Tell Henley to bring the boy and come to the courthouse soon as he gets home. Miss Sally here is under arrest." I kick and scream and cry, but they drag Mama off in they car anyway. All on account of Miss Petty bein' so nasty mean.

Daddy, he ready to cry, too, when he come home and find Mama gone. He grab my hand and we run all the way to town. To the Madison Courthouse where they got Mama. And old man Crouch is settin' there waitin' for him, just like a spider.

"What's this all about, Sheriff?" Daddy ask the man. Miss Ebbie tell me you arrested Sally 'cause you think my boy Jackson stole somethin' from Mr. Crouch there. Is that right?"

"You are responsible for any laws your son breaks, Henley. Looks like Jackson here stole a candy bar and won't own up to it." Sheriff Baxter sets back down in his chair and tells daddy to sit down too. "I could let you off with a warning, Henley, but this ain't the first time your boy has been accused of stealing from Mr. Crouch's store." He leans forward, almost whisperin' at daddy: "Your son has a little problem with sticky fingers, according to Selma Petty. Says she catches him eyeing sweets every time he comes in. And later she notices something missing."

"How she know it's Jackson that took it? And who seen him take it?" Daddy sit straight up and pull hisself forward. "Seem to me all you got is suspicion."

"That's all I need to ban you from my store," Mr. Crouch bark back at Daddy. "If Selma says he's suspicious, that's good enough for me."

"But that don't prove nothin' 'cept she just don't trust black folks from the quarter—the folks that keep you in business, Mr. Crouch." Daddy lean back slow and quiet now and wait for Sheriff Baxter to say somethin'.

"You saying you want to take this to court, Henley?" Sheriff ask Daddy.

"Is that what you want?"

"If that's what Mr. Crouch here want. My boy say he ain't stole nothin' and that's good enough for me. And Mr. Crouch and Miss Selma ain't got no proof of nothin'—'cept hate."

"Did Selma actually ever see the boy steal anything?" Sheriff ask Mr. Crouch, but the man is stubborn and tell him again Miss Petty finds sweets missing every time I come in the store.

It go on like this a while longer, till Sheriff Baxter finally tell Mr. Crouch that him and Miss Sally got to take Daddy and Mama to court and let the judge decide. Mr. Crouch yell at him that he plan do just that and slam the door goin' out. Sheriff Baxter tell Daddy he can take Mama and me home, but don't leave town. He walk us to the door and out on the porch. 'Fore we get too far down the dirt road, he call out to Daddy: "You got to know when to stand up, Henley . . . and know when to take your licks. But if that was my boy, I'd believe him, too."

It don't end there. Old Mr. Crouch say we can't shop in his store no more and Mama and me got to walk three miles now to get groceries. Daddy say he wasn't goin' give no more money to that store nohow. And when everybody in the quarter hear what happen, they all walk the three miles, too. They ain't happy 'bout it, but they know it's right. Sheriff tell Daddy not long ago that old man Crouch on hard times now he ain't got no business from the quarter. I think about what Mr. Crouch say to me last time I seen him, 'bout stealin' bein' the same whether it's a nickel or a hundred dollars. I think about them chicken necks and the sign in the window. And I think about how that nickel candy bar he say I took is now done stole away all his business, and it make me sad somehow.

ARIEL KAPLOWITZ
FORGETTING

when my grandma sees me she says
oh honey you look good.
last time she said
she's not a looker but we don't mind. she doesn't remember that.
i try not to either.
one time she said donna you've gained weight.
one time she said don't let him hold the baby.
one time she said how about a cold drink?
one time she said how about a cold drink?
one time she said how about a cold drink?
    we said no each time. sitting in dust & mottled things, sunken
    couch. uncle's old trophies. ceramic bowls with candy wrappers.
    something rotten in the sink. i creaked with shame, fear.
    we winced each time, winced for wincing. we turned to brick.
the fridge was warm. no cold drinks.
she couldn't find the car.
forgot where she put her
keys/wig/hands.
forgot lipstick,
said to the mirror oh i am an old frog. wig askew.
clung to my grandpa, familiar face, those turtle cheeks, muffled throat.
i picture her brain with cheese holes in it. she looks blank
around the room, eyes minnows. nervous. we loom around her,
darkhaired strangers who ask her about her yesterday
and she says what day? she says lovely, lovely. everything's fine,
clutches table with white knuckles. jaw gritted shut.
i sit next to her, help her find the bathroom.
every so often i say hi grandma, to remind her
so she doesn't have to ask -
saves us both the rush & blood.
she says oh honey, you look good,
and links her arm in mine. leans on me when we walk.
her weight surprises me.
she is heavy.

Rebecca Pelky
THE THING

If hope
is a thing
with feathers,
she is also

heavy,

ostrich-large
and egg-bound

with lead,

land-bound,
head
above the sand,
but sinking.

Jamie Horten
COMBATING CONSTITUTION

Luminescent beams of ultraviolet heat were permeating the air
around us, so much that it seemed as if the horizon were dancing like
a transparent candle flame, yet we pressed forward without thought.
There was room for nothing else, only the mission, because unless we
carried on there would be nothing else for us. The two of us had the
best view in the Humvee, through the gunner's hatch on the top. Being
centered, I could see everything for miles around, and Constitution,
my rifle, was pointed forward, ready to cut down anything within
550 meters. It was a perfect partnership. I carefully watched, and
he patiently awaited my need. We could see the silver truck crest the
horizon in the distance, not far from where Constitution pointed, yet
he gave me no sign of danger. It was such a common occurrence that
I barely took notice as the truck drew closer. There were constantly
cars or trucks on the road, rebelling against the warnings we had been
spreading for days. The truck seemed just like every other vehicle,
giving no indication otherwise-until it crossed the double yellow about
500 yards in front of us, straddling both lanes.

From that distance I couldn't see the machine gun mounted in the
bed, but I could see the man who jumped out of the passenger seat and
climbed on the back. By the time the Humvee stopped, I knew what
was about to happen. My neurons all started firing at once. My heart
was frantically attempting to escape through the veins in my neck. I
was poised, finger on the trigger, aimed down the sights, fully aware
of what I needed to do. I could feel Constitution in my hands, almost
vibrating in anticipation of the shot.

I embraced the moment, ready for whatever might come. A thousand
thoughts of what would be crossed my mind in less than a second, but
of all the possibilities, I didn't expect a moral conflict would take hold.
It was as if my finger was suddenly cast in lead. Try as I might, I simply
couldn't complete the series of actions so well practiced to take down
a target. No, it wasn't Constitution; he had never let me down before.
He was ready and willing, just as he always had been. It was the
unseen children of the father in front of me; the cries of the wife to the
husband I held in my sights; the father that I knew would forever live
in sadness if I took the life of this man's son. I couldn't do it.

Suddenly there was a flash of light and a line of smoke from behind a few large rocks at our three o'clock. It went directly into the side of the truck; paused, then disappeared in the massive ball of fire and smoke that took its place. The Marines had come in from the side and eliminated the threat, and I was left to wonder what would have happened if they hadn't.

This thought was like poison in the mind. Had the Marines not been tailing that truck for a few miles before it stopped, Constitution and I would never have walked away. I couldn't understand it. For what seemed decades before leaving the states, all we did was practice together and train. So much that Constitution had become an inorganic extension of my body. There was very little conscious thought involved in placing five out of six holes in a three centimeter circle of paper 25 yards in front of me. Shooting at paper was easy. It didn't show emotion; it didn't flinch at the sound of a rifle; it didn't have the portals to the soul staring back at me as a man does. What I learned in that moment was profound; even though we had put in the time together: I suddenly couldn't depend on Constitution to keep me safe.

I had allowed myself to succumb to the general bias that soldiers are simply pawns, trained in the art of war without heart or soul. Suddenly the introduction of a contrary belief shifted the war raging around me to a new war raging inside me. Constitution was supposed to be my best friend, confidante and the only real thing I could depend on in combat. It was engrained in basic training that our rifle would never be farther than an arm's length from us, but suddenly I was revolted by the idea of carrying him. I didn't want that responsibility or power; it felt inhuman to hold life or death on the foundation of personal choice. There I stood, in a position of mortal danger, afraid to use the tools of my trade. I was stripped of my comfort and naked to the enemy until I could resolve the tension between us.

Over time I've come to realize that this tension is the only thing protecting me from transforming into some kind of diabolical fiend. I had seen the type before: men who had let the supremacy control them, using force to establish dominance with the power of weapons. These types were rare, but dangerous. Holding a rifle would change them into something power hungry and uncontrollable. More often than not, they would end up in prison or some mental hospital working out their inner struggles with professionals qualified to bring them back to the realm of sanity. Without this subconscious struggle, I could easily have slipped into this type of thinking simply by embracing the relationship I'd developed with Constitution.

But true soldiering requires the ability to challenge the personal quandary of using a rifle to protect oneself. I was the father of children; I was the husband to a wife; I had a father that I knew would forever live in sadness if I allowed my life to mean less than the lives of each man who opposed me. The same was true of my soldiers... I couldn't let them down. In the heat of the moment, survival is the only thing that matters, but how does one man justify the death of another? Each man or woman must find the balance between the need for protection and the potential consequence of destroying human life. I feared Constitution, but I learned to respect that it was my choice to use him. We kept each other safe for a total of over two years in the face of the enemy, constantly finding ourselves in situations of peril. Instinct and fear drove me to use him when the need would arise, but it was never without conflict of morality, the very same conflict that almost cost me the ultimate price.

Kirk Westphal
PAPER CHURCH

I pray inside a paper church
and print my needs and sins
on walls of gossamer translucence
between Within and With All.

I write them on the inside walls
setting free each time a sparrow psalm
to flitter in the rafters,
maybe build a nest,
safe Within
and guarded from the winds
of would-be absolution
that might froth away
my dandelion confessions
just to be replanted.

Still sometimes I ask for rain
to run the ink, to blur the words
from inside out,
stains to be gathered
by With All.

KIRK WESTPHAL
ASKING FORGIVENESS

Fractured hummock ice on the bay this morning
any rifts that open, grey
A deepwater ship moored in frozen months
points toward open water beyond,
a compass needle, knowing.

A shorebird on the beach
could not wait long enough
and perished by the edge of hunger
or of North Wind off the bay,
now a carcass hull
becoming its own ribcage
like the old ships.

The belly of the ship groans
at ancient captive ice
knowing it has not begun to tremble
and it must before it cracks and yields
to bow waves breaking once again
across the dust of days.

Patrick Kindig
THE #1
for Lansing

snorts and sighs, stopping outside
the hospital parking garage on whose turrets
a schizophrenic perched

some years ago, visible across the street
from the classroom in which I was learning to decline
German nouns and heroize Icarus

not for his flight but for his fall, his final accession
to gravity. People enter, tired,
carrying bags of books, groceries, empty

pop bottles, looking for a way to get
where they are going that is more reliable
than wings, one close enough to pavement

that a fall from some hydraulic tongue
would bruise rather than break, scrape
rather than shatter. And the #1

offers this, its clozapine route straight
and regular, running from the great white Capitol
to the university, past the KFC

where a boy was indifferently shot
and the house where my brother
was robbed while he showered, past the street

where my best friend grew up
to be pistol-whipped for his wallet,
its path looking from one angle

like the city's insistent backbone,
from another like a row of stitches
sewing the asphalt shut.

SARAH LAYDEN
DON'T LOOK NOW

The image pops up on my screen, and I click for the larger view. There is my college boyfriend in his wedding kilt, escorting an ecstatic blonde woman down the aisle. They fulfill all the wedding clichés, appearing beautiful, happy, in love. She looks friendly and open, a good match for him. I wish them well, though it would feel awkward to tell them so: I was not invited to the wedding, nor specifically sent the pictures. They arrived via social network, via mutual friends, and all I had to do was log on. I did not choose to access this imagery or information. He and I are not even connected as online "friends." A single picture appeared, and I made it bigger. Then I proceeded to click through whole albums. The family toasts and wedding party. It was like I was there, 2,000 miles away.

I didn't have to look. But I did.

That's how I found out my other college boyfriend was engaged to be married this year, too: simply by logging on to Facebook. I've never met his fiancé, but I've seen her in a bikini. When she tags her betrothed in status updates, the two of them scroll together down my news feed. They are deeply interested in alcohol, and food, and what alcohol to drink with what food. If I had a glass of champagne in my hand, I'd surely raise it. They are only 1,000 miles away, but I wasn't invited to their event, either.

That's the way things work, as they should. Neither of these men and their plus-ones made our wedding guest list eleven years ago. I wasn't in contact with either one. This was pre-social network, pre-instant access to our daily lives and constructed soap operas. Which isn't to say I didn't think about them among our guests—especially the ex who dumped me—witnessing me as a bride, aglow with the kind of happiness that incidentally would cause him wistfulness and regret. As if I were somehow lacking in attention (I wasn't), I pictured how various scenarios would unfold. It occurs to me now that I was projecting. Imagining being seen, when I'm the one who cannot look away.

*

This problem—and it does feel problematic—carries some history. Consider the black-and-white photograph from high school that I keep buried at the bottom of a box. My friend on the yearbook staff gave it to me, and I was relieved it didn't make it into that year's edition. It's a crowd scene of a cute couple at a football game: they sit close together, intent on the action on the field. She wears a big, floppy, early-90s bow in her hair; he's in a rugby shirt. They are holding hands.

The only other person in focus sits five rows up in this crowd of hundreds. A girl in a Pixies t-shirt topped with her dad's flannel, also wearing a jealous open-mouthed scowl, staring directly at the couple. Looking like a much more awkward version of Kristen Stewart, and in dire need of a haircut. Do I need to tell you that girl was me? And that I had a raging crush on the boy in the rugby shirt? And that my friend who slipped me a copy of the picture did so while laughing hysterically, aware of the shame factor in its exposure? I remember seeing the photographer pointing his camera at them, though I didn't know I'd also make the shot. I could've focused my gaze on any of the boys I was with, in a large group of friends where dating was a possibility. But my eyes didn't abide such logic, nor my brain. I looked. Even when it made me feel badly, I kept stealing glances.

Something in me must love to squirm, to nearly make myself sick with what I've seen. Like a rubbernecker at an accident site. Or worse: the times I find myself not recoiling but purposefully noticing roadkill, plentiful in Indiana. Friends and I used to joke that it was National Roadkill Month, no matter the month. Growing up near wooded areas and rural roads, we were surrounded by death. Stagnant, roll-up-your-car-windows, flattened death. Unmarked and unburied. Raccoons offering up their stiff hugs. Possums with insides like strawberry Jell-O. Squirrels—those crazy, impetuous monsters—that had it coming to them, tails now their thickest parts, still waving in the breeze of passing cars.

"If it's gross, don't look at it," my mother once snapped from the front seat of the car, irritated with my loud, childish disgust over something smushed on the center line. I managed to stop complaining, but couldn't stop looking.

Now I live in the city. A couple summers ago, a raccoon was hit by a car and landed on the grassy corner of our busy street, where it would remain for weeks. I crossed to the other side to avoid smelling it, but I kept glancing over to see its progress, its liquidizing, its fur worn away.

Rib bones emerged like white plastic, perfectly curved. Eventually I strolled by instead of crossing the street. The grass had flattened and yellowed into the raccoon's tubular shape. Technically, the remains lay on city-owned easement. But how could my neighbor, who is a professional landscaper, stand this in her yard? Possible, yet hard for me to believe: Maybe she did not see it.

*

We know how difficult and painful it is to look at death. It took me a long time to understand the benefit that the open casket provides the grief-stricken. This is one way to understand: to see for yourself and know that the person inside that oblong clamshell really and truly is not among us, not in the way we are used to. We are different from them. We can move forward, live our lives complete with sandwiches and toothbrushes and insomniac wanderings around the house at three a.m. My grandparents in repose: looking rested, if artificially so. A distant cousin, her hands and fingers badly bruised from clutching the steering wheel. The beloved friend, whose body couldn't make it to the funeral: for years I searched crowds for his face, his gait, his peculiar and inimitable smile. That mouth I'd once kissed. I hadn't seen proof of his death, so maybe he wasn't actually dead. I kept looking.

*

When I look, it is out of curiosity. Or need. Or want. To try to understand all that has come and gone. Lately, thinking about my two ex-boyfriends' weddings, I wonder what it means that they both are getting married now. They are on either coast, and I am in the middle of the country, the heartland, preparing for the arrival of my husband's and my second child. Maybe this means nothing, like the online requests to play Zynga Bingo that I keep receiving from a high school classmate, a nice girl, but one I barely knew, and oblivious to my lack of interest in bingo. Like the woeful pictures of pound pups and cats that I am too allergic to adopt. Or the complaints about parking, the workplace, your sports team's performance, the hateful thing somebody said to you that you will rise above by ignoring, forget the fact that you are paying attention by mentioning it.

No. The difference is these things mean little to me. And the ex-boyfriends? Well. There is a part of me that is content with "once" and would like to live in the present. I would like to notice what's truly important and then look away. I'm a poor fit for all the sharing, all the scrolling, all the windows into other people's worlds. Yet another part of me—the part that's always been an observer and turned me into a writer—loves peering into those windows at other lives. The part of me that would stare as long as possible if given such a brightly-lit scene on a dark night. Even if the scene made me uneasy, even if I knew I'd regret looking in.

*

I think of that narcissistic wish we all have, to varying degrees, of being seen in a particular way. Via an easily manipulated tool like a social network, we can present ourselves in the best possible light. No dressing room fluorescents here—we're all spotlighted in a flattering, soft glow, sometimes with the help of PhotoShop and Instagram. We are the ceremonial wedding in stiff clothing and straight postures and whitened teeth, not the dinner over the kitchen sink and the tight-lipped negotiations over bills and the shared glances over raised champagne flutes. We are the heavily made-up and stylized body in a casket, not the bloodied, unattended roadkill.

Both are real. One is more real. These pixelated manipulations keep death at arms' length. We can live forever on the Internet, and can be forever young and flawless through the images we select to represent ourselves. Scroll through your social network of choice and observe how few people use a current photo as a profile picture. In denying that we're aging and changing, we commit the ultimate act of human hubris: imagining that we can cheat death.

"Don't look now," we say, when we really do want to engage a person's gaze, but only after a delicious delay. When we share our lives through the filter of a social network, there is only delay, no "now." Forget your fast network speeds: projected to the audience is a self that has been manipulated and released via an intermediary. Working to find meaning —true meaning—becomes harder. We have to dig through additional layers to seek out the real.

It used to be our brains doing this work in isolation, constructing meaning specific to who we are and what we see. A memory of what once was equals a vastly different thing from a life that now is. Like anyone, I have a particular set of memories associated with people I knew in the past. The brain appreciates these designations, leaving space available for the new. Keeping up with past loves and friends and acquaintances floods my brain, muddies the waters. It is, to use a word Facebook has branded into the collective consciousness, complicated.

I don't particularly want to follow my ex-boyfriends' forays into marriage, home ownership, kids and pets and whatever else they wind up with, though I know I'll fail to avert my eyes when I come across the information. While I do post photos from my (present) life, the thought of sharing pictures online from our own lovely, memorable wedding day leaves me feeling vulnerable, uncomfortable, exposed. Those versions of ourselves weren't raised in the pose-n-share generation. Our wedding photos don't exist digitally. And what's more, I don't want to compare our lives and see how they stack up, or to imagine how I am being viewed. "Compare and despair," says a friend of mine about Facebook, and I suspect she also offers a gentle warning. But to cut off all ties, to sever those links? Or to use technology to "hide" people from online sight, in which case my curiosity multiplies and then I seek them out? This feels even worse, like deliberately spying. How are we different, how are we the same? It tires me. It ties up my imagination. I want to put my brain to better use.

*

In a post for online journal Thought Catalog, Liz Colville offers "20 Things You Don't Have to Do on the Internet." Among them:

> 14. You don't have to use a social media tool the way everybody else is using it, or the way the creators of that tool want you to use it.

> 19. You don't have to look at pictures of your exes on Facebook.

Freeing sentiments, but I can't help but wonder: What will it take to make me look away? Horse blinders—or its equivalent, special software—to block social networks? It's not disconnection I want. I believe our online interactions carry significant meaning and value, and I use the technology daily. As more time passes, though, I understand that richer meaning and deeper value comes from what we see literally before our eyes, in real time, where the only intermediary is the optic nerve sending images to the brain.

Perhaps what I seek is a candid moment, a flub or ad lib that goes off the script. Not necessarily seeing people in poor lighting, but at least seeing them as they are: real, not a representation, and cast in natural daylight. Barring what would most likely be an awkward reunion, I'll miss out on those things. Perhaps that is as it should be.

I know what I will see, if I happen to embark just a few miles in any direction from home. I'm imagining a summer day, driving down a ribbon of hot asphalt , and coming across what was once a live animal in the wild: more road kill on the gravel shoulder of a woodsy route. No one has dressed it up or laid it out or slapped makeup on it or PhotoShopped it into a funny pose or made a snarky remark after having time to construct a snarky remark.

This is real. It is grotesque and unpleasant, and it's not so much that I want to look but that I can't help myself from seeing. Don't look now, I might think, but of course I do look. Right then in the moment, and later, in memory. This is real. I am witness to it.

Here. Now. I want to see.

CHARLES MALONE
LUDINGTON
from Lake Michigan Lighthouses

I want to say it is impossible to hold a baby and remain self-centered.
On some mornings the clouds tear open but the rays do not penetrate
                                        glass meaningfully.
My mother died on Christmas Eve and I will never use cancer as a
                                        metaphor.
Some of Haydn's compositions are unpalatable in this season.

The endless digital stream of baby photos was taken in the sun.
Some climates, literal physical climates, are not conducive to activism.
It is possible to wear a tie to work while devastated.
All the things and all the people at once tearing through brightly.

There are wonderful events that when put into words seem horrible.
There are nurses.
Clouds settle over language; specifically, Amiri Baraka died.
Haydn died in May; the opening to his London symphony almost fits
                                        this moment.

All roads and sidewalks are slick with slush as we gather.
You can go days without seeing the sun here.
Like a trumpet concerto; not like someone who sees the world well.
To feel absence and absent simultaneously may be dangerous.

This accretion is a mess. Layers shuffled, splashed together. Ice upon ice
gathering against the folded blade of steel at the mouth of the harbor.
There are Mediterranean plants in the Euphorbiaeceae family the same
glacial blue. I would never recognize the similarity because
of the absence of white. The absent absence. The ground is frozen. I am
unrooted. I want to crawl into a warm house away from everyone like a
damned Dutch colonist. I know better. Experiences press against some
internal breakwall. I know to push back with music and poetry and
movement. I run across the bleak to a tall metal slide on a playground.
It is the kind we expect to have disappeared for safety reasons. Lungs
pump. Like a relic from childhood. Climbing and descending and trying
the swings in the biting wind and colorlessness is enough to
hold the world together. In the summer the ferry can take you to the
other side.

KATHLEEN MCGOOKEY

LIGHTHOUSE TOUR, SOUTH MANITOU ISLAND

Lake Michigan heaves its slow heartbeat on the sand. The tower
narrows the higher we go. My son stomps on each lattice metal step
and sand from his shoes sifts through. The tour guide stops our
group on each progressively smaller landing, asks, *What part of this
lighthouse was built first?* and, after we've climbed through a trapdoor
that disappears into floor, *What happened in this room?* I don't lean in
or look down. My daughter tugs her braids and asks for my camera.
The guide offers a story: here, two older brothers watched their
parents' boat go down in a storm. A little light, extinguished, while
the lighthouse blinked *I'm here*. At the top, we are allowed outside.
It'll be windy, the guide says, *so take off your hats*. I glimpse a thin
railing and reach for my children. *If you drop anything*, the guide says,
just let it fall.

Rebecca Pelky
RIVER, TRIP THE LIGHT

The paper birch peels itself
for kindling, for rafts and words,

and the ice, the small rounds
of breaking as he pushes through.

The undertow shuffles me
toward rushing, his hands

scoop sand and hollow bones
on the fire, so what's left

of gull and glass meets ember,
his fingers, deadfall, just stone stairs

tumbled by wintergreen,
cedar saplings in limp chimneys. This

is a broken oxbow, and a loon
is howling from some edge of open water.

Bruce L. Makie
FROM WHERE I STAND

I'm not prepared for this. I had stopped thinking of her, even thought that I wasn't in love with her anymore. I'm in the city to see my family and pick up supplies and Judi Soberman is standing in the checkout line in front of me. My mother had said not to shop here, the store will have nothing I want. The place has gone to the dogs, she said. But I've wanted Judi since eleventh grade. A large man buying lighter fluid and orange juice is standing between us. I make myself small.

There are ten or so others in line. A man in back is kvetching about a loaf of bread. "We tried that," he says to his wife. "It doesn't toast well." I turn to see the woman close her eyes and her lips tremble, as if she is counting silently, or praying. The man reaches for something from the end cap special, a flashlight with batteries, and places it in their cart. The woman puts it back. "Live in darkness then!" he thunders.

Judi turns around, sees me and forces a smile. She's been crying. Her father is sick, she says. Maybe dying. *She needs me*, I think. I forget, for an instant, my pain, the shopping list of regrets; it seems so selfish. Then I feel cheated that I cannot now ask: why? Why the unreturned calls, the unanswered letters? Seven years since I last saw her, at the time of my own father's death. She held me tight then, but when I tried to call her in the weeks that followed—nothing. I was grateful that she had come to see me. Only later resentful. She never actually said good-bye.

I tell her that I'm sorry about her father, and we turn to our places in line.

An older woman in front of Judi is returning an outdoor lounge chair— it's fall already—telling each of us that it is unused. Or like new. A young man asks the woman how she's feeling today. He wears a stylish suit, scarf and a fedora that only a certain kind of man looks good in. He's lean like a stick of gum and his world seems an easy fit.

"*Nu?*" she says in a rich accent. "How do you expect me to feel carrying this?" She says that she's running out of time. She has a bus to catch. That she is tired.

"Why don't you lie down on that thing," he tells her. "I'll get you a pillow." He laughs. "I'll even read you a story."

The woman grips the chaise with both hands, holding it off the floor and erect. "I don't want to use it," she says.

"*Bubeleh*," the man says. "It looks used to me."

He toys with her and I don't know why. I suppose every checkout line has its asshole. Still, I want to watch their small act play out, keep it between Judi and me. But then the woman turns to me, as if for an opinion. I start to turn away but not before I see a small burn hole in the orange webbing where the chaise folds in half.

"It's like new," she says again. Then looks me over and asks if I ride the bus.

Judi touches my sleeve, as if to say let it go.

My grandmother once mentioned Judi's father to me. It was a matter of money, or business, perhaps neither. A favor here, a misunderstanding there, some ruffled feathers still fluttering in the breeze. My grandmother didn't give up grudges easily. She packed them tight like pistols and if you were wrong and in her sight, mercy to you.

She didn't recognize me this morning when I walked into her room at the nursing home. She's going blind, and had taken refuge beneath her covers where I found her. She confuses me with my cousins. I shouted in her good ear that I am Hencha's son. She answered that her roommate steals from her, and asked how many grandchildren she has. Her memory spins like a roulette wheel, stopping here or there: the dry goods store in Hamtramck; am I married? Her once tight jaw is slack with age and from it spilled sentences one part English, one part Yiddish as if, like a long distance runner nearing the end of her race, she draws unconscious strength from equal measures and so must pace herself to the finish. When I said that I must go, she gripped my shoulder, slowly pulled herself up and leaned back on the headboard. "I'm not so happy to be alive," she said. It was the same acid tone, tinged with irony and sadness that she might have used twenty years ago to say, *You know, you really should listen to your mother*. I said good-bye and was in the corridor when I heard something in Yiddish I didn't understand.

But dying doesn't trouble me, not my grandmother's, or Judi's father's. Not even my own father's anymore. Why should it? I turned thirty-two last week and my death is impossibly far off, like a bus inching its way along the horizon of some foreign backwater. It's out there, but moves to no published schedule. That's all I know. When it comes, so be it. Plenty of seating. No, death doesn't bother me. It's whether I've loved enough.

Judi dotted the i in her name with a circle and when I first met her, in journalism class, the dot looked as big as a heart. I thought maybe it was. I don't remember having the courage to ask her out, but there we were, sixteen and seventeen-years old, looking at a movie guide in my father's Olds. The guide fell, and retrieving it, I accidentally brushed her leg. I had this great crush on her and thought that she liked me too, but I was afraid to tell her. Afraid to hold her hand, or kiss her. We saw "The Dirty Dozen" at the old Mercury Theater on Schaeffer Avenue in Detroit.

The woman with the return is indignant and resolute and denies to the cashier that the chaise lounge is used.

The man with the orange juice and lighter fluid asks, loudly, why there is only one register open. "Dumb fucking chair," he says, and I nod. He storms off.

The cashier takes the woman's receipt. He looks desperate but his voice is controlled and measured as he interrupts Elvis Costello on the PA to page the manager. He tells us he's sorry, there's nothing he can do.

Those of us left in line exchange sideways glances. We shuffle our feet. It's as if we are all on pause, trapped in an elevator, waiting to push a button to somewhere. Even the music fails to resume. Nonetheless I transport myself to another place, another floor, a nonexistent one where I can make a different sort of purchase. The be-all and end-all of personal care products. It will go on like hairspray, and be called Fear-not. Merely touching Judi's knee that evening in my father's car terrified me. From then on I ran—it seemed the safe thing to do—from every woman who ever liked me. *Adios*. One word. And easy to remember.

The music plays on. The old woman pockets her money, yet lingers for an instant. She tells the cashier that she knows he's busy so she'll put the chair back. Aisle three, she says. Below the cat food. The well-dressed man in the fedora reappears like magic to gently lead her away, and I think better of him.

Before stopping here I visited my mother. She said why go there, they were out of business. "Yes, I'm certain, it was in the Jewish News a month ago." She waved at the bookshelf where magazines and newspapers were neatly stacked. "None of the owner's kids had any interest in it. It became impossible to find anything. Stock was piled everywhere, like garbage. All of it a mish-mash of times gone by."

"Or of times to come," I said, and she laughed.

My mother laughed often, yet rarely smiled. I took off my jacket. Though the slider to the balcony of her second story apartment was open, the heat was on. I knew that these things were connected: Her razor-thin comfort zone, and enduring efforts to not tip the scale one way or the other. Her maddening guile to demand restraint from others that was so circumspect in herself. The head-back, deep-throated laughter and singular inability to smile freely. The draft, and the furnace.

Seventy and in good health, her big unit flourished while the secondary parts sputtered. "The store isn't safe," she added, which seemed preposterous. "They don't have anything you want."

She started to discuss her will, worried about leaving one cent more to one child than the other. She'd rather be dead first than do that. "What's fair is fair," she said. I told her that I didn't come to discuss the will.

"You think someone's going to shout you instructions from my grave?" We were drinking coffee in her kitchen. She wore a bright tailored three-quarter sleeve silk blouse that seemed to compliment her fading strawberry color hair. She touched my wrist. I stared at the spots up and down her arms that had turned her skin into light mocha.

"You do not get things back in this world," she said. "You just move on."

She slid into reverse anyway and asked me about every single Jewish woman I knew. Or thought I knew.

"Do you ever see Christina Bumgarten?"

"Tina overdosed."

"Nancy Goldman?"

"Ugly and disagreeable." I changed the subject and thanked her for the birthday check, enough to cover a month's rent.

"I didn't much like her sisters, either," said my mother, and laughed. "Rebekah Stern?"

I didn't answer. My mother and I were used to long silences between us, they'd come and go like open water when the ice breaks up at sea. Neither of us was ever in a rush to jump in.

"Will you ever marry?" she finally asked.

"I'm not the staying kind."

"Maybe you haven't met the right woman." A pot of water boiled on the stove. I imagined a frenzy of bubbles rising to the surface, each bearing yet another wish for her children.

"Maybe. And maybe I find leaving more attractive."

"Why do you say that?"

"The door always looks good."

Judi is almost to the front of the line.

We dated once or twice in college. The last time I saw her there she was deeply saddened too and I didn't ask why. What bothered her then? I wonder now, watching her. I want her to know that I never stopped looking for the right words.

I got my degree but I never learned how to talk. At least not to women. Perhaps we didn't talk enough in my family, among ourselves. My mother and grandmother (who lived with us) were each cut from the same cloth; you sailed alone, and kept your business to yourself. Feelings were seldom discussed, and self-sufficiency topped their charts. I became self-sufficient, all right; I whisper sweet nothings into the bathroom mirror at night, then reach for whatever pills there are within. When I can't sleep, I go outside—I live in the country, in the middle of nowhere—to watch the stars and when I see one fall, I think that's the life for me.

"Is there anything else?" The cashier asks Judi. She shakes her head. Cash or charge, the clerk asks. Judi says cash. "We don't use plastic," she adds. Plural, I notice. She's married now.

Credit I have, but with whom? That is what I'm thinking, watching her. I have missed the boat. My wallet is stuffed with plastic dreams. She cannot see the regrets that pool in my throat, make it tighten, the words swimming with nowhere to go. I'm dizzy and my heart races but it makes perfect sense and I must tell her that love, too, is merely an act of credit. A contract. I'll honor my pledge, and you believe that I will. Judi lives without credit and I without her and it all seems so futile. I want to tell her this, that love and credit are the same, but I say again how sorry I am about her father.

She bought a disposable camera. What in God's name does she want to preserve of this time? I know there must be an explanation. I want to give her advice on perspective, make some joke. I want to laugh with her. I want her to love me like I thought she once did, and prove to her that I have so much more to say now than I did years ago. I want to hold her, or just not let go. It's all mixed-up inside. I need to shop some more, I want to tell her. Please don't go just yet.

We're in the parking lot. In the painted hills that surround us the splash of fall colors is cleaved neatly in two by the highway. A bus approaches. Judi moves toward her car. There is little time.

"Wait," I say.

Compressed by too much time, my words erupt and flow like lava. Everything pours forth: our imagined lives together, and the years apart, empty like those black spaces between the stars. Yet it is oddly still too, as if I am watching the two of us from on high: Judi is standing near me, yet at a distance beyond measure. My legs shake wildly, as if exhausted from the pitch. I stare down at them, at my words, too, detached and unswerving as they rush by in chunks bold and bright. Judi reaches out to touch me, though not without caution. The wind catches her hair, makes it swirl upward like an eddy of leaves.
The bus rounds the corner and comes to a stop. Judi can't hear a word I say and steps back. The driver inches closer to where I stand. The doors open. The old woman is sitting up front with the chair. She flashes the money she got back at me. She has both the chair and the money.

"Help me get it up there," she says, gesturing to the shelf overhead.

I step up to help her. Inside the bus smells like burning leaves, only different. Empty rows of patchwork seats stretch away from me as far as I can see.

I grab the chair and the woman smiles, an impish turn of her grey and whiskered lip. "What's a burn hole between friends," she says.

"This isn't the way I came," I turn back to reassure Judi, but the doors close. I see her mouth the words good-bye. "This isn't the way I came," I tell the old woman.

TREVOR ARNETT
REBUILDING THE OCEAN

I

For you I drink vodka straight
and build porticos to greet you.
        I am living it up.

I find myself fitful in forests
lamenting the enchanted.
I host pageants to trumpet your voices.

In funhouses and ghettos
I gild subterranean hovels
I weld beaches together to memorialize tea dances.

Because of you
        I unlock my toolbox to pummel memories. Whatever I do
        I do it blithely
        I hammer, nail, and gather sharp tools together
        I file my chisels
        to carve out the ocean.

II

For you I'm dreaming.
        Princes stepping over bones, sailors, young men
        on yachts waving.
        For you I'll build monuments to drifting.
        For you I'd rebuild the waves.

For you I whispered *storm*
and knew one was coming.

III

I travel long distances to southern locations.
On vacation I poke holes in my eyes to see stars.
    I dive in dark water to scratch names at the ocean's bottom.

I swam naked in dangerous waters, in Puerto Vallarta
and Morocco I started to gamble. For you I dealt hearts
though knew well you were losing.

I garner new lovers and use them like soap. I feel up loss and finger pity.
  I lift heavy weights
to keep you in my arms.
        I built crosses and platforms
        to prop you up as if using my hands were enough
        to hold back the hurricane

    At funerals I buried memories.

IV

These days I don't think of the ocean.
I'm blind to the thinnest horizon. I heckle ephemera
and walk backwards to see my footprints in the sand.

I am alone on the beach.

    I smile precariously and laugh in church.

        For you
        I walk into sculpture gardens
        to touch the patinas.

In the backyard I build colonnades
and bring you crumbs at night.
In winter I keep windows open
to welcome you inside.

JAKE MORAN
IN THE BASEMENT, YOU'RE HUNTING

for a way to say *loneliness*
without being dramatic but something more
like a cat in a half-sleep

dream on your lap, like tea
you drank too hot from the cup
with the painted loons, and before

any time at all you'll speak
to them very calmly, politely asking
come back up from the lake

or sea or whatever season it is,
they've been there long enough
to set your arms trembling

with *visible are the wreaths of minutes*,
your thoughts aching for a flight
of stairs like a poem where a tangled mess

of hair is the perfect nest in your perfect
amber throat, always holding something

you should have swallowed or else spoken.

Marc Sheehan
WINDBREAK, WEST MICHIGAN

For warmth against
the cold dress
in layers, memory

of first love
over wool, over
flannel the fur

of field mice
nesting your basement.
Then something to

cut the wind –
nylon, Jäger, or
line of arborvitae.

In the spring
they'll find you
leaning east, bent

but unbroken, rising
from this glacier-scoured
landscape that has

you by the roots.

CONTRIBUTOR NOTES

KAREN ANDERSON earned a MA in English Literature from the University of Michigan. For 30 years she wrote a weekly column for the Traverse City *Record-Eagle* and published two books of her work. She now contributes weekly commentaries to Interlochen Public Radio.

TREVOR ARNETT received a BA and MA in English literature from the University of Michigan. He is also an oil and watercolor painter with a BFA from the Pennsylvania Academy of the Fine Arts and an MFA in painting from the University of Minnesota. He has taught the visual arts at the University of Minnesota, the Flint Institute of Arts, and the University of Michigan, Flint, as well as secondary level English, Spanish, and French.

*ELIZABETH ARNOLD is a graduate of the MFA program at the Rainier Writing Workshop. Her work has previously appeared in such places as *The Gettysburg Review, The Whitefish Review, The Superstition Review*, and elsewhere. Her essays have been nominated for a Pushcart Prize and been listed as notable in *The Best American Essays*. She lives on a working farm in Central Pennsylvania with her husband, horses, chickens and dogs.

*TREVOR GRABILL has spent his life wandering around the Great Lakes states and now lives in Kalamazoo, Michigan. His work as Flat Mountain Press includes drawing, printmaking, and writing in the service of various clients and ideas. He's exhibited work in Michigan, Minnesota, Wisconsin, New York, and California and was recently an artist-in-residence at ISLAND's Hill House in East Jordan, Michigan. He also spends time petting animals, watering plants, going for long walks, and thinking about the weather.

*DAVE HARDIN is a Michigan poet and painter published in *The Carolina Quarterly, 3 Quarks Daily, Hermes Poetry Journal, The Prague Review*, and *ARDOR Literary Magazine* among others. The poem "Blank" was written at the 2014 Bear River Writers Conference and read aloud there for the first time.

*DIXON HEARNE lives and writes in Mississippi. His short fiction has been twice nominated for the Pushcart Prize and earned numerous other honors He is the author of several recent books, including *Native Voices, Native Lands* and *Plantatia: High-toned and Lowdown Stories of the South*, which was nominated for the Hemingway Foundation/PEN award. Other work appears in *Oxford American, New Orleans Review, Louisiana Literature, Cream City Review, Potomac Review, New Plains Review, Louisiana Review, Big Muddy, Roanoke Review, Wisconsin Review*, and many other magazines, journals, and anthologies. His has a new novella forthcoming in 2015.

*JAMIE HORTEN was born in Marshall, Michigan and is the father of four children. After graduating from Kingsley Area High School in 1998,

Jamie joined the United States Army. His 12 years of service included four deployments, one to Iraq and three to Afghanistan, totaling over two years in combat zones. His awards include the Meritorious Service Metal, Presidential Unit Citation, seven Army Commendation Metals, six Army Achievement metals, four Good Conduct Metals, and various campaign ribbons. Jamie is currently working for Munson Healthcare and attending Northwestern Michigan College, both full time.

*BRANDYN JOHNSON'S poems have appeared in *The Green Bowl Review, Counterculture, Blue Pepper, The Dandelion Farm Review,* and *The Puritan.* He was recently a poetry editor for Eastern Kentucky University's *Jelly Bucket* literary magazine. He is currently an adjunct instructor for Black Hills State University. He lives and writes in Rapid City, South Dakota.

*ARIEL KAPLOWITZ has had an undefeatable passion for writing and storytelling since the fourth grade. She grew up in East Lansing, spending months each summer in Northern Michigan hiking, reading, camping, and writing. She is a senior at the University of Michigan studying Creative Writing and American Culture, and besides writing, Ariel loves speaking Spanish, talking about social identity, and writing stories with fifth graders.

*PATRICK KINDIG is from Lansing, Michigan and is currently a graduate student at Indiana University. His poems have appeared or are forthcoming in *Eclectica, Bloom, Court Green,* and elsewhere.

*JOEY KINGSLEY is an adjunct instructor at Virginia Commonwealth University. She received her MFA from Virginia Commonwealth University in 2012 and holds a B.A. in English and a minor in studio art from the College of the Holy Cross. Her work has appeared or is forthcoming in *Jet Fuel Review, Mead, Salamander, Unsplendid* and *Drafthorse.* She lives in Richmond, Virginia.

*MERCEDES LAWRY has published poetry in such journals as *Poetry, Nimrod, Prairie Schooner, Poetry East, The Saint Ann's Review,* and others. Nominated for a Pushcart Prize, she's published two chapbooks, most recently *Happy Darkness.* She's also published short fiction, essays and stories and poems for children. She lives in Seattle.

*SARAH LAYDEN'S debut novel, *Trip Through Your Wires,* is forthcoming from Engine Books. A graduate of Purdue University's MFA program, her fiction, poetry, and essays have appeared in *Stone Canoe, Blackbird, Artful Dodge, Reed Magazine, [PANK], Ladies' Home Journal, The Humanist,* and elsewhere. She is a lecturer in the Writing Program at Indiana University-Purdue University Indianapolis.

*BRUCE L. MAKIE was born and raised in Detroit and has lived in Traverse City for some 22 years. An analyst with the Michigan Department of Human

Services, he won the 2012 Michigan Writers Cooperative Press chapbook contest for fiction for his short story collection *Fathers And Sons*. His recently completed full length play, *A Good Joe*, is under consideration for production.

*CHARLIE MALONE can never decide if he should live in a city and adventure in the wild or live in the wild and hunt culture in town. His writing is a product of this dilemma and has recently appeared or is forthcoming in *Sugar House Review, Saltfront* and others. He recently edited the collection *A Poetic Inventory of Rocky Mountain National Park* with Wolverine Farm Publishing; the project encouraged writers to explore their connection to land, flora and fauna. Currently, Malone lives and writes in Big Rapids, MI, where he is privileged to work with the students at Ferris State University.

*KATHLEEN MCGOOKEY has published a book, *Whatever Shines* (White Pine Press), a chapbook, *October Again* (Burnside Review Press), and a book of translations of French poet Georges Godeau's prose poems, *We'll See* (Parlor Press). Her chapbook *Mended* is forthcoming from Kattywompus Press, and her next book of poems, *At the Zoo*, is forthcoming from White Pine Press. She lives with her family in Middleville, Michigan.

*JAKE MORAN lives and works in lower northern Michigan. His work has appeared in *The Dark Mountain Project*, and his zine collaborations can currently be found at https://www.etsy.com/shop/CorrinaUlrichArt.

*KEVIN OBERLIN is a Michigan native now living in Cincinnati, Ohio, with his wife and sundry animals. He's working on a few sonnet sequences, teaching at Blue Ash College, and struggling to write a poem for his sister's wedding. His chapbook *Spotlit Girl* is available from Kent State University Press as part of their Wick Poetry Chapbook series.

*REBECCA PELKY lives and writes from Marquette, Michigan, on the south shore of Lake Superior, where she is also an associate poetry editor for *Passages North*. Before going back to school to write poetry, she spent thirteen years working as a zookeeper. Once she was run over by a giraffe, which may suggest that she's better suited to writing poems. Her poetry has appeared or is forthcoming in *Prick of the Spindle, Stone Highway Review, The Chattahoochee Review, Yellow Medicine Review*, and the Manifest West anthology, *Diversity in the West*.

*AMY SCHMIDT's poems have been published or are forthcoming in *Ruminate, Profane, Mud Season Review, Kindred* and *Calyx*, among others. She was a finalist in the Janet McCabe Poetry Prize and winner of the Jewish Literary Review's Anniversary Prize. She lives with her husband and tenaciously poetic daughter in the woods of northeast Minnesota where snow is a given and sun is a gift.

*MARC J. SHEEHAN is the author of two poetry collections, *Greatest Hits* from New Issues Press and *Vengeful Hymns* from Ashland Poetry Press. He has published stories, poems, essays and reviews in literary magazines including *Michigan Quarterly Review, Paris Review, Prairie Schooner* and many others. He lives in Grand Haven, Michigan.

LISA WAMSLEY is a small business owner in Traverse City. She writes poetry and is working on her second novel.

KIRK WESTPHAL is originally from Holland, Michigan and is now an environmental consultant in Boston, working around the world on water supply plans. He was a 2012 winner of the Plein Air Poetry Contest in Massachusetts, and his poems have appeared in *Dunes Review, The Road Not Taken*, the chapbook *Lines in the Landscape*, and National Public Radio. He is also the author of a nonfiction book entitled *Ordinary Games*, a collection of stories that suggest that the greatest moments in sports occur in sandlots or on asphalt basketball courts, scheduled for release in June 2015. He loves sharing poetry with his children, and his nine-year old daughter is also a published poet.

*denotes first appearance in *Dunes Review*

Call for Patrons

Dunes Review is a not-for-profit endeavor to promote creative work within the Northern Michigan writing community and beyond.

The cost of publication can be underwritten in part by individual contributions. Please support the publication of the Winter/Spring 2015 issue with a donation of $25.

Send your check payable to Michigan Writers to:

Michigan Writers
P.O. Box 2355
Traverse City, MI 49685

Thank you in advance for your support!

DUNES REVIEW SUBMISSION GUIDELINES

Individuals with current Michigan Writers memberships ($40 annually, which includes a two-issue subscription) may submit work at no cost. If you are not a current member of Michigan Writers, please use the General Submitter category on our Submittable page ($5). Or, join or renew your MW membership. Learn more about MW and the benefits of membership at michwriters.org/join.

All submissions received during the reading periods will be read. The response time will vary according to the number of submissions. We make every effort to respond to all submissions within four months of receipt. If you have submitted work via dunesreview.submittable.com and have not received a response within four months, please contact us by email at dunesreview@michwriters.org. Our next reading period runs from October 19, 2014-January 15, 2015.

All submissions must be submitted via dunesreview.submittable.com. We do not **accept submissions via email or regular mail.** You will need to have a submittable.com account to send work, even if you have previously submitted to *Dunes Review* using other methods. Creating an account is free, and you can easily keep track of your submissions from within your account.

Please submit no more than one submission in a given genre while a decision from us is outstanding; multiple submissions sent in the same genre will be unread. Simultaneous submissions (the same pieces sent to multiple journals) are permitted. Please withdraw your work from Submittable immediately or contact us via email if the work has been accepted elsewhere.

We consider:

- short fiction & essays (up to 3000 words)
- poetry (3-5 poems; please format & submit as a single .doc, .docx, or .pdf document, one poem per page)

We do not accept:

- unsolicited reviews
- unsolicited interviews
- snail mail or email submissions (please use dunesreview.submittable.com)
- previously published material

The Fine Print

When submitting poetry, please group 3-5 poems in a single document and then upload your submission. Do not submit your poems individually; doing so will make your poems appear as multiple poetry submissions, which will not be considered.If you are interested in submitting translations of literary work, please query the editor (dunesreview@michwriters.org) before submitting. The translator is responsible for all author and publisher permissions regarding the source work.

You agree to be added to *Dunes Review* and Michigan Writers email lists when you submit. You may unsubscribe from these lists at any time.

Payment for accepted work comes in the form of two copies of the printed journal.

Publication rights notice: Work published in *Dunes Review* may be reprinted on our website's Archives page. Otherwise, all rights revert to author upon publication.

The regular submission deadline for our next issue (19.1, Winter/Spring 2015) is January 15, 2015. Please "Like" us on Facebook and receive notices for upcoming events and public readings.

WILLIAM J. SHAW MEMORIAL PRIZE FOR POETRY

This contest is open to all Michigan residents (including part-timers) living on or north of the US-10 corridor. Submissions should include a cover letter providing name, address, telephone number, email address and the titles of up to three (3) poems. The deadline is February 1, 2015. A $10 reader's fee for all contest submissions will be required when you submit; further details are available on our website. Thank you in advance for sharing your work with us!

SUBSCRIPTIONS

We encourage you to become a subscriber. To receive two (2) issues, or to give a gift subscription, please send your name, address and a check for $20 to: Dunes Review, P.O. Box 2355, Traverse City, MI 49685. Alternatively, become a member of Michigan Writers ($40 annually) and gain access to other benefits as well as a subscription.

For more information about Michigan Writers membership, activities and events, please visit www.michwriters.org.

MichiganWriters

Made in the USA
Charleston, SC
29 September 2014